SIGNPOSTS FOR LIVING

A PSYCHOLOGICAL MANUAL FOR BEING

DR KIRSTEN HUNTER

BOOK 1
**CONTROL YOUR CONSCIOUSNESS –
IN THE DRIVER'S SEAT**

BOOK 2
UNDERSTANDING MYSELF – BE AN EXPERT

BOOK 3
**MINDFULNESS AND STATE OF FLOW –
LIVING WITH PURPOSE AND PASSION**

BOOK 4
**UNDERSTANDING OTHERS –
LOVED ONES TO TRICKY ONES**

BOOK 5
PARENTING – LOVE, PRIDE, APPRENTICESHIP

BOOK 6
NAILING BEING AN ADULT – HAVE THE SKILLS

A MEANINGFUL LIFE

DEVOTE YOURSELF TO:

1. **KNOWING** YOURSELF,

2. **LOVING** OTHERS,

3. **LOVING** YOUR COMMUNITY,

4. **GRATITUDE** FOR THE MOMENT, AND

5. **CREATING SOMETHING** THAT GIVES YOU MEANING AND PURPOSE.

First published 2021 by Kirsten Hunter

Produced by Indie Experts P/L, Australasia
indieexperts.com.au

Copyright © Kirsten Hunter 2021

The moral right of the author to be identified as the author of this work has been asserted.

Except for the purposes of reviewing, no part of this publication may be reproduced or transmitted in any form or by any means, electronic or mechanical, including photocopying, recording or any information storage or retrieval system, without the written permission of the author. Infringers of copyright render themselves viable for prosecution.

Cover design and image by Zach Lawry @ Mates Rates Screen Printing & Design
Edited by Jane Smith @ www.janesmitheditor.com
Internal design by Indie Experts
Typeset in URW DIN by Post Pre-press Group, Brisbane

ISBN 978-1-922742-10-0 (paperback)
ISBN 978-1-922742-11-7 (epub)

Disclaimer: Any information in the book is purely the opinion of the author based on personal experience and should not be taken as business or legal advice. All material is provided for educational purposes only. We recommend to always seek the advice of a qualified professional before making any decision regarding personal and business needs.

To Jon

PREFACE TO THE SERIES

This series of books is actually a conversation that I have had with thousands of people over the last twenty years of clinical psychology work. From approximately 42,000 hours of conversations with clients of all shapes and sizes and from all walks of life, all struggling during their various stages in life, I have learnt so much. When you have the same conversation that many times and you see progress, you see where the value lies. I want to share this conversation with you.

'Signpost for Living' is written out of sheer frustration and exhilaration in equal measure. I have limited hours with my clients. This series of books is the information, across the breadth of 'being human' areas, that I would cover with clients if there was no limit to time. This is my 'ideal situation' series, to share with others how to understand and master ourselves. We are pretty dodgy at being human. We really have very little clue about how we work – we don't fully understand our emotions, our behaviour, our neurology, our physiology – or how to live with purpose, calmness, contentment and joy, with our loved ones and within ourselves. This series covers all of these life-challenge hotspots and things we need to learn about ourselves. If we get support, encouragement, and general guidance in these areas, we can get on track quickly. Life can expand and boom us into more contentment and happiness.

How amazing life is if we allow it to be.

If you get a new puppy, it is wise to put in the time to train it; you can enjoy your pup so much more once it's trained. Your pup becomes easy and fun to walk, reliable on your carpets, and an enjoyable character. This is strangely true for *us* too. By studying our thinking, emotions, behaviour and styles of relating to others – really getting a solid level of self-awareness and having a robust skillset – we can enjoy ourselves and our world so much more. And no, we do *not* need to be puppies to learn new tricks; we can learn as adults, at any stage of life. No excuses here. It is absolutely, profoundly, exasperatingly ridiculous that we do not all learn this information routinely at school. 'How to be human, class 101'. Humans have the code to develop physically, but we need more information to develop psychologically into full adults. Not learning these basic life skills can leave us feeling insecure, disconnected and unsafe.

Life is growth. Life is a work in progress.

This is what these books are about. We do not know everything about 'being human' – far from it – but we do know a fair bit. This knowledge, which comes largely through the profession of psychology, is not, however, common knowledge. And yet it should be. It needs to be. We need a manual for being human, for without it we are driving blind.

This series is based on clinical evidence and sound reasoning. It provides clear, calm direction – not all the answers, but solid signposts. Time to share this knowledge with everyone.

WHAT TO EXPECT IN THE 'SIGNPOSTS FOR LIVING' SERIES

The books in the 'Signposts for Living' series are independent but complementary; by strengthening and cultivating one area you enhance all of the other areas simultaneously. There is not much point fixing one hole in the boat when the other holes are not receiving attention. This is not a piecemeal series. We need to cover the whole of human functioning. In this series there will be chapters you need, chapters you don't, chapters that talk to you now, chapters that will tap you on the shoulder in your future. The 'Signposts for Living' series is written for everyone: all ages, mums and dads, grandparents, young adults and teenagers finding their way.

The books are broken down to first explore (in Book 1) how controlling your consciousness can help you grab the reins to your nervous system, thoughts and emotions. Relevant side-alleys that are common traps to dodgy thinking are included. We then flesh out your personal issues in Book 2: *Understanding Myself*. The importance of being awake in life and aware of your present moment is celebrated in Book 3, along with the gem of living with purpose and passion in a state of flow. 'Signposts for Living' then broadens in Book 4 to discuss understanding our relationships with our people (the good, the bad and the ugly). The true complexity of parenting is then dissected in Book 5. Finally, the art of nailing being an adult is fleshed out in Book 6, revealing the excitement of reaping the rewards of becoming a thriving mature human.

To make the books as concise and user-friendly as possible, I have avoided references, footnotes and other scholarly tools as much as possible. The goal is for you to be able to access and use this valuable information without feeling bogged down or needing to have specialised, background knowledge. To acknowledge my sources and guide you to delve deeper, if you wish to, I have included 'further reading' lists where relevant at the end of each book.

Welcome to understanding your humanness.

BOOK 6
NAILING BEING AN ADULT – HAVE THE SKILLS

'Adulting'. It is a skill. Below is a breakdown of some really crucial areas to get your head around and check that you are on track. It's a mixed bag of areas. If you are not skilled in these areas, it's time to up your game. You will reap the benefits and your life will launch forward when you master these skills.

CONTENTS

CHAPTER 1	ESSENTIAL FAILURE: OUR FRIEND	1
CHAPTER 2	HEALTH: TAKE CARE OF YOURSELF	5
CHAPTER 3	YOUR PHYSICAL ENVIRONMENT: WORLD, HOME, WORK	22
CHAPTER 4	LIFESTYLE BALANCE	28
CHAPTER 5	SUFFERING, GRIEF, STRESS	35
CHAPTER 6	SPIRITUALITY	44
CHAPTER 7	APPRECIATE CULTURE	48
CHAPTER 8	HARD DECISIONS	50
CHAPTER 9	CIRCLE OF KNOWLEDGE: THE WISE PERSON IS HUMBLE	55
CHAPTER 10	MONEY	58
CHAPTER 11	MASTERING PROCRASTINATION	64
CHAPTER 12	NO ENTITLEMENT	73
CHAPTER 13	INTERNAL STOCKTAKE: WHAT DO YOU SUBSCRIBE TO?	76
CHAPTER 14	OPEN PALM	79
IN CONCLUSION		81
FURTHER READING		82
ACKNOWLEDGEMENTS		84
ABOUT THE AUTHOR		86

CHAPTER 1
ESSENTIAL FAILURE: OUR FRIEND

Failure is essential to life. How could we possibly succeed if we never fail? Failure teaches us what to do next time. The key is always to be open to learn from our failures through being self-reflective, and to own our responsibility. We need to be brave in order to extend ourselves, and we need to persist when we face challenges. Perhaps most of us give up too early. Life is about hanging in there and persisting with our principles, our ambitions and our resolve.

Life involves trial and error, mistakes and consequences, and periods of licking our wounds. But from these difficult times in life – our crash points and our crossroads – we learn, we grow, and we become skilled at life. The key is to accept these difficult times as exactly that: just *times* in our life. Times that will pass, and that we will survive and strengthen through. The key is to not panic about our hard times, but accept that this is where we are right now, and that working through it is our job. Emotional pain is very much like physical pain. If you can understand it and calm and distract yourself, then your attention towards those pain pathways is minimised and you can keep on top of it.

But if you panic about the pain, then you focus in on it, and it flares up even more and you become utterly overwhelmed.

When clients come into my practice in absolute grief, then of course I support and empathise with them, and I skill them up to get through it. But quietly I am excited for them, because I can see what's ahead. They usually come in with life problems that have built up and festered for a long time, and *now*, due to their crisis of emotional pain, they are ready to make significant change. They are ready to grow and strengthen and re-navigate their approach to life, so that finally they can move out of this previous pattern of dysfunction. Just as a builder can visualise the exciting outcome of a house renovation, I feel exhilaration in seeing the life alterations the client is capable of achieving. I can just imagine the relief, the joy and the empowerment they will feel. What is more exciting than that? I swear, I have the best job in the world.

Nevertheless, when we are launching into new adventures or extending ourselves beyond our comfort zones, we all feel fear. With expansion often comes fear. You can't accomplish anything truly meaningful without risking failure. We learn many lessons on how to get things right by first getting them wrong. What valuable lessons they can be, those lessons that require failure – and yet we fear failure.

We also need to make our own judgements about success and failure, and not be concerned about how other people evaluate what we are doing. This is challenging for our fragile egos, but we cannot line ourselves up to jump through everybody else's hoops, only our own. Gentle mentoring through these rough times when we fail is extremely valuable. Without support and guidance, we as learning adults might not gain strength from our failures, but just stay knocked down. People who are on track with aspiring and positive growth have had just as much failure in their lives as those who are struggling, but they can stop and study their life's crash site to learn about themselves and skill up for next time. This is the skill of resilience: the inner assurance and the capacity to bungee back. Failure is not the issue; failure is inevitable. It is our capacity to grow from it and back ourselves that is important.

> Our failures don't limit us,
> only our *fear* of failure does.

It takes courage to be prepared to fail. To have courage we need to be open to vulnerability and this possibility of failure. It is about doing something when there are no guarantees: telling someone how you feel, investing in a relationship, being brave enough to share your private needs and issues. It takes even more courage to pick yourself up and build a stronger foundation once you have failed.

Failure is not something to be fearful of or ashamed about. It is a crucial part of learning and strengthening. It is an amazing thing to become familiar with fear and our sense of vulnerability regarding failure. When we can identify, understand and respect these emotions, we can tolerate them and let them wash over us and then move forward. We can then make decisions based on wisdom and not based on fear. Actually, we can make our life choices *despite* fear, because we do not fear the fear. We do not fear the failure; we know that we will grow, rebuild and strengthen. Failure can be our friend.

CHAPTER 2
HEALTH: TAKE CARE OF YOURSELF

Here's an interesting thought: when we have children, we reflect on how we are going at parenting; when we have pets, we reflect on what kind of owner we are; if we are an employer, we (hopefully) think about how well we are managing the ship ... but as a adult, do we stop and reflect on how we are going with looking after *ourselves*? How are we going at being an adult and guiding ourselves? This section is about creating a time to reflect and to find clear direction for self-care. There are many areas to explore. First we will look up from our puppet strings to the world of technology.

PLUG OUT

We receive such a constant flow of online information that we need to learn the skill of having boundaries with technology. The online world constantly floods in; our boss can access us anytime by email; our friends and family can reach for us whenever they want. We have no 'island time' to be unavailable, or to not be plugged into the world.

Having 'boundaries' here means reducing the tide of data that we toggle over, and creating time and space to be off the grid. Some examples of boundaries may be to check your emails only twice a day and to train people around you that you are not available 24/7. My family follows the rule of no technology when sharing a meal, or when talking with people. At home we have a technology tub where devices live and charge; this removes temptation when our boys are needing to switch off from the tech world.

LOTS AND LOTS OF STUFF

Have you noticed that when you have fewer possessions, you have a quieter mind? Life is simpler when you are not the caretaker of a lot of 'stuff'. You can streamline your environment and you are off-duty from managing a more complex home environment.

The temptation to accumulate things is always there. But when the happy buzz of the initial purchase passes, we can end up working to pay off our gear. An alien would look down and observe that our stuff is the master, and we are the workers. Strange, isn't it? How many hours of our working year are spent paying off stuff that lost its value as soon as it left the store? Then in time it is just *stuff* – stored, thrown out or barely worth selling. We also have to manage how to live with it all around us; we become a storage unit.

After all, the simple things like sunsets, a hearty laugh, and a good wine are far more soul-fuelling than possessions. An emphasis on things can distract us from the ability to enjoy the simple pleasures that actually matter. Simple pleasures give us a release of pressure from societal status; when we enjoy them, we don't feel the obligation to compete, to have the latest toys, to be perfect, or to jump through the hoops. We can relax and sit, and let go of our control, our grip, our chasing of our tails.

SELFISH TO SELF-CARE

Some people feel selfish if they take care of themselves. They resist taking time and energy for self-care. They feel that they are undeserving. This usually stems from unhealthy and unbalanced lessons in early life that taught them that self-care is a selfish act. We learn to 'be generous towards others, not ourselves'. But you actually have a *duty* of care to yourself. You are your own responsibility; nobody else has primary responsibility for you. Just as you are responsible for looking after your physical health, you are responsible for your psychological health and your happiness.

HONOUR YOURSELF

If a child was in your care, how would you look after that child? You would not let them just eat rubbish; you would make sure they ate nutritious food. You would give them sunlight and exercise, you would understand that they need sleep to enable their brains to function, and you would take care to ensure they were clean and well-presented. You would prevent the child from experiencing exhaustion and depletion.

You are that child! You are as important as that child, so use the same mindful and intelligent approach. You would have high standards for that child, and those same high standards apply to you. You need to love and look after yourself, not kill yourself slowly by neglecting to care for yourself. We need to take an active role in our own self-care and in improving our overall wellness. This is about honouring your body and your mind.

Great actions speak great minds.
– from *The prophetess* by John Fletcher and Francis Beaumont, playwrights

MIRACLE BODY

Part of valuing our health is appreciating when we have good health and not taking it for granted. Our bodies really are extraordinary. From our ability to digest food and release our bowels, to our ability to walk with co-ordination, see, hear, smell, feel touch, talk, think, have balance, move oxygen through our bodies, and hundreds more examples, our bodies are capable of amazing things. We need to appreciate how wonderful and miraculous our bodies are.

I severed my anterior cruciate ligament in my knee while swimming in the surf. My leg felt like a puppet limb that was dangling out of place. Through six months of recovery, surgery and then recovery again, I came to appreciate my knees, my legs, and my capacity to walk, to drive, to be independent, to carry things (once I was free of crutches) and to exercise freely. I am so glad of this injury because my appreciation of and relationship with my body are now really positive and on track. I am now motivated to regularly exercise, mainly because I *can*, and I celebrate this.

Often we take things for granted until we lose them (relationships included!). There is a golden life lesson in this.

LEARN YOUR BODY

It's great to learn about your body. Your body is unique; what works for it and how the body expresses stress varies from individual to individual. Through being mindful of your body, you can learn what your body does and doesn't need in order to thrive. You can learn how stress and anxiety are expressed in your body and mind. You can even learn how to process pain and discomfort, so that you do not escalate it, but acknowledge and then move your attention away from it, so as to distract your pain receptors. Rather than feeling betrayed by our bodies if we are in poor health, we need to be gentle and accepting towards them. We need to befriend our bodies. We need to trust and support our bodies in our capacity to heal, learn about ourselves and grow in our understanding of how the amazing machine that is our body works.

It's interesting that health brings us happiness not through actually *having* good health, but through our *perception* of how healthy we are. It is our appreciation of our health that counts. Even when we are sick, being able to keep the ill health in perspective is the key to coping with illness. We cope better if we understand that healing will come and we appreciate the good health and functioning of the rest of our body. We can stay afloat and have a positive appreciation and outlook even through chapters of ill health. This is applying the skill of being **adaptive**.

BODY SCAN TECHNIQUE

The body scan is a wonderful way to get in touch with your body and mind. It is an investigation into the moment-to-moment experiences of your body. You bring awareness to whatever you feel or sense in your body. This acknowledgement helps to work with stress, anxiety and physical pain. Life has us focus on our future and our past; we are often preoccupied with our thoughts and our stressed imaginations. This technique will help to bring our awareness to our experiences within our bodies instead.

Here's how we do it.

We move through our body, concentrating on each part, bringing our awareness to how that part of our body is feeling. As we work through each of these areas, we focus on relaxing and 'dropping' the pressure out of these parts. We start with our toes on our left foot, scanning up our left foot, part by part: left foot toes, foot, ankle, shin, calf muscle, knee, thigh muscle ... then the same with our right foot: right foot toes, foot, ankle, etc. We then work through from our buttocks, internal organs, back (lower to upper) to our shoulders, and then work up our left arm (fingers to upper arm), our right arm (fingers to upper arm), then return to our neck and our jaw, the top of our head, and forehead. There is no need to do anything about your sensations; just *feel* them.

You are learning the wisdom of your body. The feelings may be pleasant, unpleasant or neutral. You may notice a wide range of physical feelings like aches, tingles, itches, pain, heaviness, lightness, coldness or warmth. Your physical sensations, thoughts and emotions are all linked together. You are discovering a more comprehensive understanding of your human experience. Body scanning allows us to 1) take time out for ourselves; 2) become aware of how different parts of our body are feeling; and 3) create a mindful release in these body areas. It is lovely.

HEALTH FORMULA

What if there was a formula that you could live by that could propel you into enjoying your health more, almost like a maintenance schedule to make the engine of your life purr along contentedly? Well if there was, it would include these four cornerstones: exercise, diet, sleep, and streamlining your headspace. Let's have a look at these cornerstones now.

Exercise

We can use exercise to reduce our stress response. When we are stressed, that part of our nervous system called the **sympathetic nervous system** swings into action. This can be triggered when we are experiencing stress, urgency or any level of fear. Any movement, particularly walking, will ease the hormone surge that is released from this spike in stress. The 'hyper-drive' hormones produced by the sympathetic nervous system are given an outlet through this exercise, and so we calm down, and our mood becomes stabilised.

Exercise is our natural and very effective alternative to anti-depressants. When you are anxious, gentle exercise is preferable to hard-core exercise. It is really important to reduce the stress reaction in our bodies. When we live with high levels of stress, we also live with high levels of the hormone cortisol and the **neurotransmitters** epinephrine and norepinephrine (chemicals in nerve cells that transmit information from one nerve to the next). These villains take energy away from our immune system, which is clearly not good news. It leaves us vulnerable to ill health and with a poor ability to heal. Exercise helps us to come out of this hyper-stressed overdrive. When you exercise you create a calmer, more playful mind, and when you give yourself time out from your mental traffic, your body will reduce its experience of stress and will recharge itself.

Exercise can also be restorative and therapeutic in overcoming previous trauma or difficult life stages. We know that trauma can lead to actual shrinking in parts of the brain, and from this it can cause a reduction in mental and social capacity. The reverse is true also: *the brain can recover through repetitive positive experience*. This is the phenomenon of **neuroplasticity**. Repetitive and positive exercise is one of the interventions that can lead to healing of the brain. This is why exercise can be one of the most important factors in maintaining and restoring mental health (as well as physical health, of course).

If you notice stress in your body, then you are experiencing the connection between your mind and your body. This connection goes the other way too. Instead of just relying on medications anytime we're sick, sad or scared, we also need to cultivate inner resilience in dealing with stress, illness and pain. The practice of formal mindfulness as discussed in earlier books in this series is also an example of how repetitive positive experience can create mental healing.

Many people speak of exercise and meditation as being their therapy, their healing, and they are absolutely accurate. Through exercise, we can also become more emotionally protected and buffered from further stress and trauma in our lives. Exercise may indeed be the single greatest thing you can do to improve your happiness. Regular exercise has been found to be more effective than sleep. Exercise also reduces many other health risks as well as anxiety and depression; for example, weight-resistance training decreases the probability of developing conditions like dementia.

We need to keep our brain and body active if we are to stay flexible and young. Human beings are not sedentary creatures; we are built for mobility. It is important to establish good, healthy habits now, so that you are set up for when you get older. You have to live in your body, so it makes sense to create a body that is vital, powerful and exuberant. Through exercise, you build your energy. Don't let yourself get into the habit of stagnating mentally or physically; this will just be another bad habit to break in the future, and you won't reap the enormous rewards throughout the bulk of your life.

How do we find the drive? What are our authentic motivation triggers or anchor points? We need to figure them out. Why do we resist getting up and moving? To find out, we need to examine what is motivating us at those times when we *do* feel the drive to get up and exercise. What can we harness from this information?

For example, I find that exercising when I don't have a deadline is essential, because I can't enjoy it if I have to be back at a certain time. I therefore only go for a morning walk on the weekends, and on weekdays I enjoy walking in the evenings. I find it a calming release. I go with Jon and the boys, and it is a time to talk and connect. When I go for a run, I only want to go on my own; it is 'me' time. I find it motivating to record my time and to gently challenge myself, and I enjoy being lost in music. I like having a set path to follow, so that I do not need to make decisions and I can relax. I am also motivated by the need to look after my leg muscles to support my previous knee surgery. This concrete, clear goal is more motivating to me then a general 'for fitness' motivation. When I can squeeze in a bushwalk, I'm in heaven.

That is *my* exercise formula. What makes *you* tick? What draws you to exercise? What is your formula for motivation? Do you need scheduled group exercise, or do you prefer solo time? Do you prefer set times (like group classes or a personal trainer appointment), or do you prefer a more flexible, spontaneous approach? Are you more likely to exercise for pleasure, or are you more outcomes focused (measuring times and reps)? Do you prefer to rely on others to motivate you, or are you self-motivated? If you have not worked out your winning formula, then you are shooting blind – which is a problem, because exercise efforts are famously shortlived, with motivation waning and procrastination winning. So, work out what works for you and lock it in.

Exercise routine is just that: routine. It is the challenge of just turning up. We need to create several windows of time per week to sweat and build strength. Choose something you enjoy so that you are much more likely to do it consistently as part of your lifestyle. Many sixty-plus-year-olds wake up each morning and have vigorous, long walks; they are limber, fit and lean, and they defy age. They are clear that this is their favourite activity and time of the day.

Try a 'just turn up' approach. In this approach, we have to create and respect limits. For example, you might not exercise if you have chest congestion, but if you just have sinus trouble it's fine, so you *just turn up*. You might go out in a drizzle of light rain, but not in a downpour or storms. Migraines, or a need to rest an injury will see you stay home, but otherwise you *just turn up*. This is about taking away the question of 'Will I exercise?' Skip this procrastinating conversation with yourself, and just do it *because it is your routine*. Your exception limits are set, so within them, just go. Once you have just shown up, you're set; you will find yourself in your exercise groove.

It is important to be mindful and pay attention to exercise as we are doing it, as this maximises the benefits of the exercise. In doing so, we are aware of our technique, we have more enjoyment, we are intentional in our actions, and therefore we have the best outcome. We are listening to our body's wisdom about overdoing it or underdoing it. We are moving our body with awareness.

Diet

Just as we can 'people-watch' at the airport, we can 'behaviour-watch' as we reach for food for comfort. This question of mindful or mindless eating was covered in Book 3, Chapter 9. Through mindful eating, we can see our patterns; perhaps when we are tired, stressed, or upset we can observe ourselves craving for and reaching for comfort food. We can watch ourselves trying to drown out our discomfort with chocolate, biscuits or cake. This is about acknowledging what we are doing. We are shoving food on top of our distress. Are we food addicts? Well, the question is *how strong is your compulsion to eat*? And if you don't comfort eat, *how lost are you*?

Our bodies become addicted to sugar pretty quickly. We crave glucose, the body's easiest energy to dissolve. Apart from causing unwanted weight gain, this sugar plays havoc with our gut bacteria balance and causes chronic inflammation. The ripple effect is enormous; all of the secondary problems just continue to roll out. This is not to mention that a diet based on sugar is an inadequate diet; if we indulge in a sugar-rich diet, we are not feeding ourselves adequate fuel. Sugar provides an empty energy hit; it does not grow or nourish us.

We need a gentle and kind lifestyle with food, not a rigid diet. Psychologically, we need to feel positive in our relationship with food if a healthy diet is to become a long-lasting routine. The focus is on what we are *doing*, not what we are *not* doing. Focus on the abundance of good food that you *can* eat. Research this food and learn more sexy recipes; this is a time for positive growth and expansion of your food world. Negative blocking and restrictions just make us focus on the forbidden fruit. This is why with a particular food we never say 'never'; we say that it is a 'sometimes-rarer' food. What does self-flagellation do anyway? It distresses us and it demeans us ... and as a result, what do we want to do to soothe ourselves? We comfort eat. It's a vicious cycle.

Eat a well-balanced, nutrient-rich diet. Real food that actually feeds your body. Highly processed white carbohydrate is one step back from sugar. It does not fuel your body and could be a weight-gaining timebomb. Your body cannot do its job of rebuilding when it is fed artificial ingredients and empty calories.

It is worthwhile to study what foods work for us. We are all unique in our genetics and biochemistry, our anatomy, our metabolism and our nutritional needs. We need to mindfully examine what our bodies are telling us as we experiment with different foods. Do you feel better or worse after a particular food? Have you tried an elimination diet to methodically experiment with your body? The FODMAP diet is great for this (ask your doctor!). How does your stomach react to particular foods? And your bowels, your skin, your heart rate, your energy levels, your head(aches)? If you can imagine the food not having many steps from the farm to your door, then it will have nutrition loading. Look for a colourful plate; colour equals nutrients, as a rule of thumb. And replenish the sixty percent of your body that is made of water. Drink water. You cannot drive without fuel in your tank. Our fuel is nutrient-rich food and water. Take it seriously.

Sleep
Having enough sleep is one of the most powerful techniques for stress reduction. We need to be sensible with our sleep. Make sure you set a routine and get enough sleep. While it is recommended that adults get seven to nine hours, we are all different, and you need to work out what your batteries need each night to recharge. We need to put ourselves to bed each night so that we are set for our tomorrow.

Sleep can be elusive and beyond our reach when we are stressed; we need to clear our minds. It is smart to get off screens an hour before going to bed. We can get our thoughts out of our heads by writing them down. Create a routine of having a shower and winding down. If the weather permits, perhaps get a heat/wheat pack and put it on your ankles to relax you and relieve your muscle aches. Focus on this experience of relaxation. You can do an evening ten-minute formal mindfulness technique to quieten your mind, as described in Book 1, Chapter 39. Go to sleep thinking about what you are grateful for and find things that you are looking forward to in your tomorrow.

Streamline small decisions

There are two reasons to pare down our decisions and create a more streamlined and efficient life. The first reason is to do with stress, and the second is to do with saving our resources for what matters.

When we are anxious, making choices becomes very difficult. We struggle to make decisions because our sympathetic nervous system is switched on; we are in threat alert, and we therefore are not using the more advanced executive functioning part of our brain that makes decisions. Basically, we don't have the neurological resources to make decisions when we are stressed and anxious; at those times, we are shockingly bad at making decisions. We get overwhelmed, we don't trust our judgement, and our minds are not able to focus. This difficulty in making decisions even makes our anxiety worse.

Secondly, we have so many important decisions to make in our day, that we don't want to waste our attention, time or effort on small, silly decisions. We need to streamline the mundane, small stuff. Many people have routines for exercise, healthy eating, or catching up with family. These are small details that we can ritualise in order to streamline our decision-making effort and attention. We can also then experience the relief of decisions having been made, rather than wading through the fog of indecision. We can focus on what matters: things to savour, and areas of growth and creativity. We can avoid decision fatigue.

It is definitely a smart life skill to streamline our small decisions and reserve our mental energy. Highly effective people have morning routines; they don't have to make decisions each morning regarding their breakfast, their exercise routine or their chores; they just follow the pattern that has proven effective for them. For work, for example, they have a 'go to' uniform. They have found what works for them and they go with it. They save their headwork each day. This is about skipping indecision and vagueness and using your brainpower for important decisions.

CHAPTER 3
YOUR PHYSICAL ENVIRONMENT: WORLD, HOME, WORK

WORLD

Caring for the world is relevant to each and every one of us. It is relevant to our health, our quality of life, the ripple effect of stressors in our lives and our ability to have choice about our future. Judging by most people's behaviour, it is evident that many feel as if the environment is something we can take for granted and deal with later – but you know, it's a bit like being at sea. At sea, you'd make it a priority to keep your craft seaworthy. You wouldn't ignore the growing number of holes and just watch your ship taking in more water.

In reality, if we don't look after our world, we will sink. With our globe, it is us, our grandchildren and their grandchildren who will continue to see and feel the effects of our shoddy maintenance work. At minimum we should be living in a world that we don't erode; it's only intelligent.

To 'adult' well, we need to take seriously what we are responsible for. We are the caretakers of our environment, and yet we are doing a terrible and embarrassing job of it. We are failing spectacularly. We need to connect with the magic of nature with its turns, rhythms and its changes.

The public debate on the reality of climate change is over, and the focus and debate are now on the degree of urgency of the need to stabilise climate change, and how and when we will take measures to recover. There is no point focusing on the short-term economic costs versus clean energy, because there will always be short-term economic costs; this excuse could be rolled out forever. When we put climate change recovery on hold, we are saying that our needs are more important than our children's needs and *their* children's. In time it will be their planet, not ours. We humans have always been selfish and focused on the short term. But renewable energy projects and readying employment and the economy for environmental policy change should be the clear focus for the future if we are to maintain a world in which we exist at all, let alone live meaningful existences.

In getting out of the mess we are in, we need to think critically, every one of us, about our actions and the ripple effect of our choices that join and cascade together into avalanches and tsunamis of environmental damage. Let's learn and think about the consequences of the choices we make each day. What did we eat? How was it grown? Where did it come from? How did it affect the environment adversely? How did it affect animal welfare? How was it packaged? How can we avoid the packaging? Is it good for our health? What do we wear? Where was it made? Does our clothing involve child slave-labour or sweatshops? By asking these questions and having the courage to listen to honest answers, we can make small changes that become big changes as the effects ripple out. We are usually oblivious to the consequences of consumer choices, but the consumer population when united has ferocious power. Let's become aware and make better choices. Let's become good caretakers of our planet, not abusers and neglecters. It's all part of taking care of ourselves.

Most of us have lost touch with nature. We need to make nature a routine part of our lives again. Our fast-paced cities, noise and congestion have been found to have a detrimental effect on our physical and mental health. Long commutes mean an increased risk of depression. Night-time bright lights mess with our sleep patterns and increase our anxiety levels. Poor work-life balance is a fast track to an enormous scope of mental and physical problems, including cardiovascular disease.

Instead of *taking* from nature, we need to *immerse* ourselves in it. Just short periods in nature, away from the pressures of modern life, can improve mood, creativity and productivity. We need to take a break from concrete walls around us, and not be available to everyone all the time. It's an ancient remedy to a modern problem. Try exploring the wild, hiking and, if it's your style, camping or fishing.

HOME ENVIRONMENT

We are enormously affected by our home environment. When we have a home environment that is calm and joyful, and radiates positive energy amongst the people who live there, then our home will nourish us. It will be where we feel safe and we fuel up. We can then breathe out from the world's demands in the sanctuary of our home.

If the people in our home are cutting each other down and causing harm, then our home is likely to be the biggest stressor in our lives. We do not feel emotionally safe; we do not feel understood. We stay at work to avoid going home, and other friendships and even relationships become a positive reprieve from the drama and stress at home.

The physical environment of our home can affect our well-being too. If our home environment is unpleasant or cluttered, we might not find it calming or inspiring. This may depress us, which is a big problem because it may reduce our energy, morale or motivation to make our homes run more smoothly. If this is your world, then your foundations of life are crumbling, and you need to have some serious conversations to turn this around. Set yourself up so that you enjoy your home. Enjoy your kitchen, enjoy your clothes storage, enjoy your laundry, enjoy your lounge area. Enjoy – simple!

WORK ENVIRONMENT

A healthy and happy work environment can go an enormous way towards creating and maintaining a happy personal life, as we spend such a significant amount of time at work and we commonly find identity through our work roles. The truth is that many of us spend most of our waking hours at work. Increasingly, we are asked to do more work in less time, leaving us feeling stretched, unfocused, exhausted and burnt out. Our work environments, like our homes, need to be efficient and decluttered to allow our minds to work calmly and at their best. Often a holiday will help us come back to work with a fresh head and see how processes are not effective or causing problems.

It is crucial to remember that we are working with fellow humans. We need to remain human and compassionate, even when we feel pressured and exhausted. Our co-workers, like ourselves, want to feel listened to and respected. People work best when they feel safe and inspired, and have a sense of ownership over what they are doing. It is smart to create this environment for yourself and, where possible, for others. We want to work with others who are calm and focused and able to engage in higher-order thinking, not panicked, mentally blocked or unable to concentrate. So a mindful and supportive environment is an intelligent work environment.

What can you do to create this streamlined and supportive work environment? More listening (to others and your emotional self) and less talking is a good start.

CHAPTER 4
LIFESTYLE BALANCE

What do you want your days to look like? How do you want to live your weeks, that become months, that become years, that become your life? *Today* is important; it is all the 'todays' that make up our lives. We are not great at stepping back and asking ourselves whether we have balance in our todays. Are we living our days the way we want to be living our life? If not, let's start the conversation. What is off-track? What is out of balance, and what can we do about it?

Balance is acknowledging the fact that work is important, but that our home lives and connections with others are arguably more important. Yet our home lives are often where we become complacent and do not tend to be our best version of ourselves. At work we reflect on our work performance as a matter of course. How about our behaviour at home, our engagement with our children, partner, parents, family and friends?

If you are living a healthy, balanced lifestyle, you will feel it; if not, you will also feel it. If you stop and ask yourself about the quality of your life balance, the answer will stare you in the face. You may also have a gradual awakening to the fact that money is not the key to life satisfaction. Beyond providing a safety net, money adds little or nothing to our happiness. Every year hordes of workaholics come out of their work bubble and realise that their relationships are in disarray, and that they have not prioritised time with their partner or kids and therefore only have a shell of a relationship. The same is usually true with parents, siblings and friends. They wake up to the fact that outside of their work and their work identity, they have not actually created and built up their own lives. Retirement or unemployment for them would spell an existential, ego and identity crisis.

Making time for our relationships and contributing to relationship-building time in the family so that we all play our role is very important. It is what is valuable in life. It is also an essential ingredient in life to know how to have leisure and 'recharge time'. Our lives are so busy and complex, we need to refuel routinely as a priority. One reason smoking became so popular was perhaps because it created these very windows of time out from our busy pace of life. We stand away, stand still and have a cigarette. We have a stimulant, yet call it relaxing. We are lying to ourselves and we don't even know it.

Some people find it nearly impossible to take time out to relax and have leisure interests, whether this be reading, gardening, walking, tinkering, painting, fishing, socialising or whatever. Why? Because they feel there is so much to do, and they feel guilty for stopping and relaxing.

Enter the **'Protestant work ethic'**. Influencing the Western world, the Protestant work ethic is the historical religious belief that filtered down into a cultural belief that our work and our economic success were sure paths to eternal salvation. If you did not work hard, you were being sinful, and your eternal salvation was not looking good. Leisure came to be known as gluttonous: a bad reflection on your character, and dangerous. Leisure equalled sin. Think about it: do you feel guilty if you stop and do nothing in particular? If so, you have been shaped by this subconscious cultural belief that recreation and leisure are sins. *If you stop, you ought to feel guilty.* Your value is in being a workhorse – work, work, work; that is where you get your self-identity and self-worth. Holidaying or relaxing at home scares you.

But the truth is, on our death bed, we want to know that we have lived life fully. That we have enjoyed life; that we have delved into areas of life that we are passionate about. Finding a work pursuit that we enjoy and are prosperous at is important, absolutely, but more important is our connection and time with loved ones. Day in and day out, we tend to have our priorities upside down. Leisure and time with our loved ones is very important. That is living. Work and domestic obligations are important for quality of life, but they are not ultimately what life is about. We are more than mice on a wheel. We are not productivity machines; we are not going to care on our death bed about our houses being perfect or whether we jumped through the right hoops at work. We are not *just* workers. We *do* need to take pride in our work and domestic work lives, but on top of this foundation is time connecting with loved ones, the richness of life passions, and time out in leisure pursuits.

There are two big challenges to engaging in leisure. The first is finding the time, because there is *always* more work to be done. The second is discovering our interests – finding leisure activities we like to do.

Let's address the first problem: finding the time. We will never get everything done. The list keeps growing as we get on top of our jobs; we need to accept the nature of this and not see it as if something is wrong. The goal, therefore, is not to get *everything* done, but to stay on top of things enough to have a streamlined, quality life. Aim for a house that is organised *enough*, clean *enough*, tidy *enough*, and a workload that is managed *enough*, where we are on top of things *enough*. Don't try to have everything done; this is unrealistic. The skill is in tolerating the idea that there is more work to be done, but putting the tools down anyway.

If we understand the never-ending quality of our workload (domestic and in our jobs), then we can understand that life is like a marathon, not a sprint to the finish line, and therefore we need to pace ourselves. Our lifestyles need to be *sustainable*, and we need to take time out regularly to recharge. We need leisure to look forward to as we push through our workload. Many of my clients find this concept agonising. Putting down tools is absolutely foreign and scary to them. We have even had to put structure around it to make them stop their production wheel. For example, on Saturdays and Sundays, come midday, they have to stop and find 'quality of life' pursuits. Talk about a culture shock for them.

People who have lived on this production wheel are then left with the second challenge: *I don't have any interests!* This can be a confronting realisation. People often need to start from scratch and fill up their lives with things to do for pleasure, personal skills to learn, creative avenues to play with. To do this we need to be constantly looking around for inspiration. We don't need confidence that we will like something or that we will be good at it. We just need curiosity and a sense of adventure and a willingness to try new things out. Even if you go to a class and find you don't like it, that in itself is living, and hopefully you'll come away with more funny stories. It is not about getting things right; it is about having a playful approach and a sense of humour about living.

Our work is not who we are.

Leisure is about life balance. Just as it is important to be productive, it is essential to find time to play and to have stillness. When you don't listen to the needs of your body, it's easy to lose touch with your own natural cycles of activity and rest. Perhaps you need to ask others to pitch in and help around the house or at work. Perhaps you have taken to micromanaging, thinking, *It's just easier for me to do it myself*. Perhaps you need to step back and see if your approach is sustainable and not a 'sprint' approach to life. Are you taking advantage of the skills of everyone around you? If they are physically and mentally capable, everyone should pitch in. It is important to allow people around you to grow and have a sense of involvement and ownership. If you do everything for everyone, then you not only risk behaving like a martyr, but you are not allowing others to grow. You are teaching them to be dependent on you. Or maybe you need to encourage *others* to relax so that *you* can feel more comfortable taking the time to relax and have some downtime.

Often opening ourselves to new pursuits or learning to approach our work with a different, more meaningful perspective requires us to downsize our egos. We need to lessen the amount of our identity that is invested in our work role. It is not easy to change our set ways. Change can result in a self-identity crisis and make us feel very lost, vulnerable and exposed. Poor adjustment to retirement is a classic example. If we have only equated happiness with achievements, we can end up with a lifetime of being a workhorse, and *purely* a workhorse. We are living as if we don't matter – as if only our productivity matters. We can become purely conveyer belts of work output. This can be especially difficult to process in a healthy way if we have not learnt the skills of understanding our fears and our emotions and expressing them to ourselves and loved ones. We need to recognise that we are something other than, and more important than, what we do for work. We need to not rely on our work role to define ourselves. Our work needs to be an expresssion of what we do, not who we are.

CHAPTER 5
SUFFERING, GRIEF, STRESS

We all have stress and suffering in our lives. It is unfortunately a human condition. We cannot escape life's uncertainties, illness, difficulties, loss, aging, lack of control of life's events, or death.

The question is how we deal with it. Do we work to process and overcome suffering, or do we let suffering move in with us and define us and our future? It is through navigating and wading through these hard times and our own personal dark corners that we find life's meaning and our own maturity and wisdom. This takes courage. We become more warrior-like in our capacity to cope with what life will throw at us next. We can learn to be more self-reliant, stronger, and closer to our own self-awareness. By going through the dark times, we can learn to keep the rest of life's smaller challenges in perspective, and we can learn to laugh at the human condition; this is profoundly therapeutic. We can laugh at our own ridiculousness. Being terminally humourless is a sad thing.

Sometimes we can have a really tough life chapter and, from it, a big shake up; our previous worldview and all the small, societal hoops that we subscribed to are blown apart. We can look with fresh eyes and a clearer perspective. Our value system has a spring clean. This is fresh growth. This is a launch of thinking outside of society's square – a time for creativity, innovation, exploration and a voice that is more authentic to you; you become no longer a sleepwalker through life. You can learn to leave your comfort zone and face your fear of change.

Managing suffering is also an essential life skill. Many believe the goal or even their right in life is to not experience suffering. That is like expecting to go through life with absolutely no physical injury or pain. But life is not linear; it is messy. We will experience chapters in life that do not go well. Life is not smooth sailing; we will all experience loss. When this happens, we shall experience psychological pain. The key, however, is to accept that this suffering is inevitable at varying points and for varying reasons. We can also see these as opportunities to strengthen. We aspire to enjoy life despite adversity.

To heal through our times of suffering, however, we have to *do the work*. There are no shortcuts, and it is up to you; no one can do it for you. This is your responsibility, and there is no way around it. You have to find your way through it. It is through suffering that we truly develop gratitude for the gift of life. We are capable of enduring hardship in our most despairing and grim times, if we can find meaning and purpose. Victor Frankl, who survived the Holocaust not only physically but psychologically, observed that, surprisingly, the men who were more able to survive the Holocaust were actually the more sensitive men who did not resist the pain, but had the capacity to go within themselves to cope with their trauma.

When life disappoints us, this is the time to take charge of what we can control, and harness the power of our own perspective. How you relate to your grief and suffering makes a big difference to the degree of pain you actually feel and how much you suffer. The power in this is that the acceptance of the grief process actually delivers us through the psychological suffering more swiftly and more painlessly because we are less fearful of the process itself. We can feel strangely empowered in accepting the storm and actively steering our way through it, as opposed to finding ourselves overwhelmed and terrified by the process. One foot in front of the other, we walk with strength through these psychologically difficult chapters in life. The future chapters in life that restore contentment to us are our reward; they return us to some equilibrium.

Unlike animals, we humans have the unique capacity to contemplate our own death. We have a sense of time, and we have a sense of our ultimate fragility and lack of control over the bigger picture. The ultimate paradox is that we can only be happy in the time that we have in our life by embracing our mortality. Because animals don't contemplate the future, they don't get anxious in the same way that humans do. We humans are trying to control the unknown. It takes courage to tolerate uncertainty as we face the large questions of existence. It is crucial to develop the skill of maintaining perspective, and to realise that *this too will pass*. You will be okay; time will move this challenge and pain past you. There is a tomorrow. Grief teaches us about the fragility of life. It shows us that death is inevitable. When we accept this reality, we can decide to make the most of time and to find what has true purpose during our precious years.

Many may be uncomfortable with this topic, but we do need to acknowledge death to be able to live life fully. It is our discomfort with this topic that is the problem. Death ought not take us by surprise. We have to factor in death as a part of being human and the context of our living. It is part of the full picture of life, and we are deceiving ourselves and doing ourselves no favours by putting our heads in the sand with regards to death. On sheer probability, death will not reach us until we are in our old age, so I am not suggesting we fear it as being around the corner throughout our lives. More that we see each hour, day, week and month as precious, knowing that the play will eventually end. It is our acknowledgement and respect for death that intensifies life. If there was no death, life would not have value.

> Our acknowledgement and respect
> for death intensifies life.

When we experience significant loss like the death of a loved one, there are standard thoughts that haunt and harass us, stealing any peace of mind. They are often *Why did they die?* And *It's unfair!* These two grief questions actually have the same blunt answer: that the world is indeed unfair. We roll the dice and good fortune or bad fortune falls upon us; there is no rhyme or reason to most misfortune, and as a result there is usually no answer to the question of *why*. The reality is that these bad things happen to us humans and it's horrible. We have rolled the dice and had bad luck. While there is a moderate cause-and-effect relationship in many events in our day-to-day life, many of the big life variables are out of our control.

When someone in our life dies, it seems that the nature and the size of our grief typically follow one of two patterns: the typical *overt* grief that we all relate the idea of grief with, and a second pattern, more of an *inverse* grief. Let me explain. Basically, the depth of our love equals the depth of our grief. This is about how big the hole in our lives is now that the loved one is not here with us; this is *overt* grief. It is as if the depth and extent of our grief is an ode to our love. The good news is that the grief will ease, but the love will stay.

There is an image that many people relate to when they are grieving the loss of a loved one. The individual is standing at the seashore. A wave of grief comes and engulfs them, and they are spinning and disoriented.

There is no 'normal'. Then the wave goes out, and during this time they just feel numb. In time another wave comes. It is mildly less enormous, but we don't notice that because it is still so overwhelming, and again the wave goes out and we are left numb.

Over time, the waves gradually become smaller, until after a little while we do *notice* they are getting smaller. This is good for our morale, and we notice that we are moving towards healing. Nevertheless, we continue to feel immense sadness, anger, fear, confusion and disbelief during our waves of grief. There is no pattern to our emotions; anything goes. The waves continue to get smaller. We can now get our heads out of the water; we can breathe a bit. We can function. The times when the waves are out change from times of numbness to – very gradually – windows of subtle happiness. Over time, some normality and more happiness overtake our numb feelings. We are left with continued but manageable waves, and some level of being okay in between. We will always experience the grief to a mild level, but the rawness of the emotion will subside. This is painful, but ultimately a healthy process.

Healthy grief involves understanding that our loved one has left an indent, an impression, on us. They have influenced us, and we take this influence with us. Perhaps we are so in tune with our deceased loved one that we can have conversations with them and know what they would think or say. An adult child can recognise how they have been shaped by their parent, and they can feel and treasure the imprint.

Then there is the *inverse* type of grief. This is when there has not been a close and healthy relationship when the person has passed away. For example, the deceased may have been a disengaged parent with whom the adult child did not feel connected. The adult child is likely to realise that she does not miss her parent's functional involvement or emotional connection when the parent dies, because there was no depth of connection to start with. Her grief instead is for the *relationship* that was not there before the parent died. The focus of her grief is therefore actually about looking back in time and respecting her needs and her sense of loss. Hopefully she will then move to an understanding of her parent, while not condoning her parent's neglectful behaviour. Perhaps she can start to feel compassion for her parent through learning the parent's back story. The goal is then acceptance that part of her story was not having her needs met. When this acceptance can be processed, there can be peace.

Traumatic grief has a different pathway. Traumatic grief arises when we have lost someone in an unnatural way. For example, the deceased person might be very young. A parent losing a child suffers perhaps the worst form of grief. We are not really designed to cope well with this grief. It usually leaves a parent continuously wounded and limping along. I have very genuine compassion for those who are so unfortunate as to have lost a child.

Miscarriage is an extremely misunderstood grief, in that society really tends to ignore it. And yet it is real. Both your body and your mind prepare for a baby and suffer from the loss, but it is your mind that takes the longest to recover and to process. The parent has bonded with their future child in utero, they have experienced it growing, they have invested in dreams for their child's future, and then this child is gone. The rest of the world goes on around the parent, usually completely unaware that they now have deep scars and often fears about loving and connecting with any *other* future child. Perhaps one of the hardest things about miscarriage is not knowing why. Why did the miscarriage happen? It is hard to heal when we don't understand. This unanswered search for 'why' easily creates fear, as we can't stop it from happening again. Miscarriage is extremely common; up to one in four pregnancies end in miscarriage, so we really need to make room for understanding this grief in society.

Our crossroads are clearly times for resilience and courage. This is a time to be exceptional. We tend to admire people who overcome hardship. We do not choose to make role models of people who have sailed through life with little adversity. The ability to transform adversity into an *enjoyable* challenge is a skill that is even more advanced than the skill of merely overcoming it. This is the skill of transforming a hopeless situation so that we can emerge stronger from the ordeal. There is a self-assuredness in this approach – a confidence that our resources are adequate to meet the challenge we face. This is about negotiating our way through, finding alternative possibilities, adapting and remaining open to our environment. With this approach, solutions to our problems are likely to emerge. There are possibilities for growth in almost every situation we encounter. The key is being prepared to perceive unexpected opportunities.

> There are possibilities for growth in almost every situation.

The vessel that carries us through life's minefield is the capacity to love – to love ourselves, our special others, and our purpose in life. This is combined with hearty laughter along the way for all of the messiness and humanness of life. Humour is the skill of enjoying the absurd difficulties we face, rather than being dragged down by them. This journey through life's struggles is perhaps how we acquire our character. We don't just come through suffering; we *grow* through suffering and we are changed by it. Through grief we can have a perspective shift that is transformative to a small or large degree; we connect with different parts of ourselves and have different realisations. This post-traumatic growth usually involves an awareness of our personal strengths, a greater appreciation for life, and a reflection on our spiritual life.

CHAPTER 6
SPIRITUALITY

What does **spiritual development** mean? That is up to you. It is a deeply personal question. It is not something to be treated with humour or trivialised. The nature of a belief system and faith is that it is *your* personal experience and faith. But what we do know is that this is about *something bigger than you*. This is about a sense of where you sit in the big universe. If we establish a sense of spirituality, and a security in this, then we feel loved and at peace. We can feel that we are no longer spinning off in life with no anchor point.

We talk about living a meaningful life. Perhaps spirituality is finding the true meaning? A deep sense of spirituality and faith does definitely help us ground our egos, as we are connecting with things much larger than ourselves. Our spirituality takes us down a path of intense awareness of the world around us, of our personal belief system and the value system by which we live. It makes us question the very meaning of our existence and, of course, our death. It is about reflection, humility and peace.

I am amused – highly amused – when people state that they are atheist or agnostic as they turn up in their flashy car or latest branded clothes, and name-drop and brag about their constant purchases and societal hoops they have jumped through. Humans are constantly looking for *things*. They are constantly grabbing the latest whatever and behaving in a way that is pretty close to worshipping those things. In their behaviour, they demonstrate that they idolise their success, their money, their status, their social media image, their looks, their beauty. Their focus and insistence on acquisition are pretty all-consuming. How is this behaviour not idolising? It seems to me that they are replacing worship of a higher being with worship of material things. Of course, many worship both! We cannot, however, get meaning, purpose, or sustained confidence from this worshipping of materialism. We need to connect with something bigger than ourselves, and that is the point of spirituality.

As well as our spirituality, our core value system also creates a framework to guide our living. My ultimate value system is love; in fact, it is the ripple effect of love. When you love someone – your children, partner, parents, siblings, friends, colleagues, clients, acquaintances and strangers – you create a sense that they are valued and cared for. You are then part of an ongoing ripple effect of love through your immediate community and into the world. Obviously, this involves having close and deep love for your inner circle, and a caring intent towards those more distant from you, but the theme is still *love*.

When we experience love from others, it soothes us, calms us and delights us, and we can be better versions of ourselves and be more positive towards others. The ripple effect then grows and grows. I certainly thrive when I am being loved and cared for, when I feel understood and appreciated. From this I can feel my loving nature grow stronger. The ripple effect is untraceable to you, and that is a good thing, because it is *not about you*. It is about having good intent towards others and wishing their worlds to become richer from your interaction with them. What a healthy, thriving framework for living! This is what I am confident will continue to matter to me on my death bed: that my inner circle of loved ones have had a life in which I have shown them love, supported them and celebrated them. This gives them a better platform for their lives, so they in turn can also be grounded and loving towards their immediate loved ones. This is the beautiful ripple effect of love. This is what gives me joy and peace of mind.

Quantum physics has created a foundation for perhaps a universal consciousness. Science has now established that when you break us all down in the form of matter (what we are physically made of) into smaller and smaller parts, or particles, there is a point at which on an atomic level the line between particles and energy becomes blurred. Our particles (atoms) break down to such a small level that there is no longer a physical structure, but energy. On this level our energy blends with the energy of all other people and with the world around us. As broken-down matter, scientifically, everything becomes one.

And just as the boundaries between two people becomes blurred on a molecular level, people are connected on a psychological level with each other and the world.

Perhaps this links in with **life synchrony**, a concept that is understood by people of many cultures including Indigenous Australians through their Dreaming and intricate astronomical knowledge, Native Americans with the conception of creation as a living process, and Chinese with the concept of qi and an ever-moving cyclical universe which is endowed with intrinsic natural patterns. The Islamic, Indian, Thai and Andean (South American) cultures also have their unique concept of life synchrony. This is about us being part of a larger rhythm of the universe. This is about the natural cycles of life around us and how they are all interconnected – how *we* are interconnected. This is a reality that you ignore at your peril. We seek to understand this interconnection; we seek to know what it all means, and to know where we fit. When we truly reflect on this life synchrony or universal rhythm, we cannot but be in awe of the intricacy and majesty of this broader ecosystem that we all belong to. Through this reflection we can discover our meaning, and have gratitude for the amazing world that we live in.

CHAPTER 7
APPRECIATE CULTURE

Culture is our glue. Our human community cannot exist without it. What is culture? Culture is our ideas, our concepts, our stories, our human-created works of beauty and meaning, our histories, good and bad, and what's important to us about how we do things. Culture is the accumulated knowledge of our forebears.

Great architecture, music, philosophy, art, drama, poetry and religion are previous advances in creating harmony out of chaos. It is important to know that a lot of groundwork has already been prepared for us. We need to understand this about being human, and open our eyes to take in our cultures. Have a critical eye – have an opinion, for sure – but more than anything, turn your attention to culture.

The beauty and wisdom of many artworks are now available and accessible to you online, and they represent the very best of humanity. This is an amazing time for connecting with what the world has to offer you. We are looking at the lifeblood of humanity, the good and the bad, but nevertheless, it is our story – your story – and we need to pay attention. We need to live broadly and take in the richness around us: our architecture, the breadth of music, honest history, gardens, sculptures, various world views through the decades, art works, design eras, our tapestry of foods, the nuances of our cultural behaviours and beliefs.

You are part of a large, broad, rich story. It is your culture and you need to be awake to this world around you.

CHAPTER 8
HARD DECISIONS

When change happens, we typically want guarantees in order to soothe our fears. The ability to trust our own judgement and take the leap allows us to start to experience ourselves and our worlds differently. This is about joining life and responding to what unfolds; it is about getting out of our own way.

A big part of our resistance to change is the psychological power of bad habits. These habits tend to become entrenched even when they threaten to destroy our lives. Old patterns lead us to lose our sense of adventure. All accomplishments that *matter* require us to take risks. Namely, the risk of failure, as we explore, invent and extend ourselves. With a society that is so focused on fear of failure and risk aversion, we can settle in life and miss these significant accomplishments if we don't shake off this fear and become pioneers in our own lives.

> The absolute truth:
> the greatest risk is not taking any.

Because we fear change, we voluntarily impose constraints on our lives, and we lose our freedom. But when we are afraid to try things, we limit ourselves. What we long to do remains as unfulfilled dreams. We put a wall up around ourselves. We fear trying and failing and we fear rejection, so we do not try. We stay within the confines of our safe, low expectations; we protect ourselves from the danger of disappointment. Yet what we need to be is *bold*.

Think of the desire to find a partner in middle age. For most, this is too frightening; they therefore hesitate or completely avoid it. They are risk averse, but as a result miss out on experiencing the greatest of joys in life: to love and be loved.

The biggest risk is to risk our heart. How do we juggle the *risk* of being hurt with the alternative *certainty* of being alone if we play it safe? We either reach out to explore another, or we hide under a rock. Instead of seeing our past relationships as opportunities to learn about ourselves and others, and to strengthen and build character, we think of them as failures that are cause for regret. We become hesitant and wary of being hurt again. We generalise and conclude that all men and women are like the one person who has recently hurt us. The reality is that on the path to finding our life partner, we get hurt, we take side tracks with others that end up being dead ends, so we come back to our path and keep looking. This is where courage steps in: being prepared to take the risks necessary to achieve our goal, our life partner to love. It is only an act of despair to refuse to seek love.

> The biggest risk is to risk our heart.

Meaningful change is usually slow. This does not go well within our impatient society. We have been socialised to expect near-immediate gratification. But to achieve significant things and real change, we need a mixture of determination and patience. Determination is generally celebrated, but it will get you nowhere without its less exciting companion of patience. Perhaps we could call this *fortitude*, a word that has almost disappeared from our common tongue. How willing are you for change? Is it purely a wish with an empty intent, or are you prepared to give it what it needs and make it happen via the continued slog of action?

We have many forks in the road – times when we need to make a decision. Many of us fear the hard decisions, so we either make no decision or we choose the easy, unwise option. As a psychologist, I often deal with situations in which people are taking the easy road or avoiding decisions. It is scary to make a hard decision such as separating from a toxic but familiar relationship, or changing a child's school because of chronic bullying and inadequate school intervention, or making boundaries with an unhealthy friendship. We are programmed to stay with the familiar, even when the familiar is doing us harm. To make hard decisions, we need not only wisdom, but also inner strength. There is discipline in making hard decisions and accepting responsibility for the consequences of these decisions. It also requires the skill of accepting delayed gratification, because we need to put in some groundwork before we reap the rewards. We must learn to accept hard times for the sake of setting ourselves up for a healthier world – and then, and only then, do we get the avalanche of positive rewards coming to us.

We fear the hard decisions.

Perhaps most decisions are 60:40 in terms of pros and cons. They are hard to call; they take a lot of mental weighing up. We are not lucky enough to have many clear-cut decisions. If it is a tight decision that's close to 50:50 and you could go either way, don't put thinking energy into it; flip a coin, for it really does not matter. With really tough fork-in-the-road decisions, however, imagine taking one of your options and see how you feel, then imagine making the *other* choice and see how you feel. Which one is most exhilarating, and which will you regret sacrificing the most? If it is a tight decision, you are then left with the reality of grieving for the opportunity that you let go.

The truth is that you can't have it all, and you have to accept that this option is not yours to have. With all these choices comes the good with the bad. A dream house or vacation puts us into debt, a promotion brings more work pressure, a beautiful relationship brings the need to step up and be responsible for your care of the relationship. This is the paradox of life. This can be a negative, but I personally think of it as a challenge that keeps life interesting. How bored would we be if life was just smooth, handed on a platter for us? We would be like an indulged, slothful prince. We need challenges, and life gives us plenty to keep us busy.

We need to accept that we have to be the captains of our lives and navigate life's challenges. We need to have periods of transition in life. This means setting ourselves up so that we feel empowered. It means living with hope and creating our horizons, not having a hopeless approach, as if we are treading water in life. Rather than avoiding living through avoiding life choices, we need to have the courage to live well.

CHAPTER 9
CIRCLE OF KNOWLEDGE: THE WISE PERSON IS HUMBLE

The circle of knowledge is a lovely visual concept to help keep us genuinely humble. Basically, the area within the circle represents our knowledge, and the circumference represents our awareness of what we don't know.

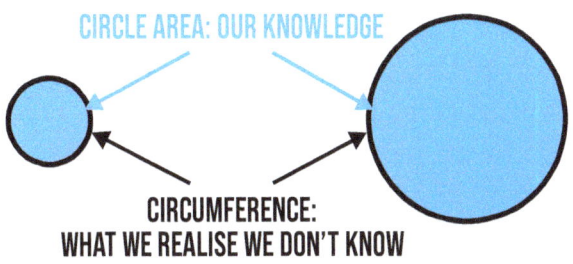

Less knowledge = Less aware of what we don't know

Larger knowledge base = Very aware of how much more there is to learn = humble

If we have a small amount of knowledge (represented by the small circle), we can be unaware of the enormous amount that we do not know, and we can be arrogant about our knowledge. The larger our knowledge, the larger our circle, and the more we realise and are humbled by what we don't know. This was perhaps Socrates' main principle: that wisdom leads to humbleness.

Let's have a chat with Socrates; he has this area covered. This is what he has to tell us:

- Mankind is made of two kinds of people: wise people who know they're fools, and fools who think they are wise.

- The only true wisdom is in knowing you know nothing.

- I know that I am intelligent, because I know that I know nothing.

- True wisdom comes to each of us when we realise how little we *understand about life,* ourselves, and the world around us.

Perhaps Socrates may have been frustrated by people on this point? Fair enough; many people seem to miss it. It is a good rule of thumb to avoid people who claim to know the answers in life. It is much wiser to be drawn to people who are trying to understand life's questions; who are curious and open to continuing to learn. They can be wrong, they can be fallible, and they are very practised at ownership of responsibility and apology. The desire to look like the all-knowing master of facts is usually a defence for actually feeling very insecure and trying to compensate for these insecurities. The secure person can stay humble and a goofy student of life.

CHAPTER 10
MONEY

The labyrinth of our issues with money, such as our approach, our priorities, our motivation, our fears, is a profound psychological area – an awkward and perhaps not very sexy topic. The challenge is not so much in having *knowledge* about money and how to manage it, but having a healthy *attitude* towards money, which is why this is a psychological issue.

Money problems are up there with our top five stressors in life. Money problems can torment us throughout life and can be the stressor that triggers extraordinary levels of anxiety and depression. Money is also one of the leading areas of relationship conflict and breakdown. It is crucial to have strong money skills in order to skip this whole financial stress spiral. Financial strength can help us feel calm and secure. We are not talking about wealth here; we are talking about financial security. Ironically, an overemphasis on wealth can actually lead to unhappiness. We need not just financial skills, but psychological skills regarding money, because this is the key ingredient. We put ourselves in a position of either strengthening our finances or spiralling down. It is crucial to get your skills on track and keep them on track for the sake of your psychological well-being.

Our goal with money: feel calm and have choices.

I'm not a finance expert, but these guidelines I've listed below are about commonsense, and I am looking at them from a psychological perspective. These guidelines, which have been endorsed by the finance people in my world, are the principles that I want our children to have securely grounded in their lives. Reading about further money management skills would be a great idea too. The book *The barefoot investor* by Scott Pape is a really useful and accessible read that has resonated with so many.

SEVEN MONEY SMARTS

Here are seven smart guidelines to help you to be in a strong financial position. As you will see, it is not about how much money comes in, but how much goes out.

1. Put needs before wants

Just because you want something, doesn't mean you can afford it. *Needs* are housing, healthy food, insurance, utilities, health costs. Putting *wants* – our shiny, fun, cosmetic things – over our needs is very dangerous. The rush of excitement from buying our wants passes quickly, leaving us in a stressed state of being unable to pay for our needs.

2. Spend within your means

It's not what we earn, it's what we spend. We need to live so that daily, weekly and monthly, our money situation is getting more positive, and we are not accruing bad debt. I know many, many people who earn a lot of money, but spend even more. So while they drive around in flash cars and earn a lot, their lifestyle is going backwards because they are spending more than they earn. On the other hand, I know many who are very modest earners, but save each week. These modest earners are literally wealthier than the big-shot earners, because they have more money in the bank. Don't be deceived by the flaunting of expensive toys: the cars, houses and holidays. Often you are seeing a symbol of debt and stress to the owner.

> *Annual income twenty pounds, annual expenditure nineteen nineteen and six, result happiness. Annual income twenty pounds, annual expenditure twenty pounds ought and six, result misery.*
> – Mr Micawber, from *David Copperfield* by Charles Dickens, writer

Holding onto your money means having the ability to say 'no' to consumer culture. Where do you spend your money, and how long does the pleasure of your purchases last? Learn not to regularly buy new clothes, eat out, or have work lunches out. If you calculate how much you spend on these things it can be scary. Where would you rather put that money? You *can* say no. Don't be manipulated by consumer culture. Take charge. At the end of each year, what do you want? More savings? More big, wow, special experiences that you have saved up for by not letting your money seep through your fingers on daily 'stuff'? Preserve whatever wealth you have. Be smart; be the tortoise, not the hare.

3. Don't abuse credit cards
Credit cards should only be used for financial emergency, unless you can clear them with ease each month. Living on credit as if it is money in your account is a really bad habit. If you did not have the money to buy something in the first place, you end up with just more debt on top of your original troubled financial situation. We can easily slide into building up an unmanageable credit card debt that we might really struggle to pay off. The banks must love this; you're their little employee earning them money each month. You have lost your financial independence to the banks.

4. Save for retirement
Feeling calm requires having confidence that you will be okay in the future. Not putting away savings for retirement is a mistake. Putting away even an extra 5% of your salary is better than nothing. Have peace of mind and protect yourself from regret.

5. Don't ignore bills
If bills are not paid on time, it will affect your credit rating, which will damage your ability to borrow money in the future. Plan and budget for bills, and pay them off.

6. Make money rewarding and meaningful

We work well when we are getting a reward from our efforts, or when we have a horizon that we are working towards and inspired by. If all of the money we earn is going to bills, we watch it just disappear, and we experience no positive reward for our efforts. Where are we going to get our drive and energy if we are just paying off debts and feel like we are getting nowhere? It can be demoralising.

So, first of all, make money *rewarding*, not just a stressful and negative responsibility. There has to be something in it for you. Put a small amount each pay day into a separate account to be used for a long-term goal: a holiday, a new bike, whatever that is. Something that is exciting and meaningful to achieve. Save this small amount before you pay the bills. We need to have a carrot; we need to get something inspiring out of our earning efforts. Seeing this money building is very rewarding. This also teaches us to save rather than spend, and to avoid putting something on the credit card only to find it difficult and stressful to pay back later.

Then, if you have problematic debts, make a plan. Get some help from a community finance education service if you need. But a good routine plan is to pick your smallest debt and aggressively pay it off first; this will give a sense of reward and achievement. Then the next smallest debt becomes the focus, and you keep working on aggressively attacking one debt at a time, from the smallest to the largest. People need to see progress to keep morale going and to maintain focus. So, make a plan and calculate a timeframe for achieving it, even if it takes a long time. The main thing is to move forward and see that eventually there is light at the end of the tunnel.

7. Stay out of bad debt

Basically, stay out of bad debt; in other words, avoid spending 'dead money' on, for example, holidays or purchases of expensive cars or furniture. At the same time, make sure good debt (that is, investment that grows your financial worth, like real estate) is manageable. If you are in bad debt, get back to being financially afloat as soon as you can and then stay there. Learn about being money smart as soon as you can.

CHAPTER 11
MASTERING PROCRASTINATION

How ironic; I've been putting off writing this chapter.

We need to just get in and get stuff done. We need to exploit our potential. Why? So that we benefit from what we can learn, build and achieve – so we can get jobs done and behind us. We are doing all of these things because they benefit us in some way. But we need to focus on reaching out and getting that benefit without causing ourselves too much heartache and stress on the way. We can only benefit from 'doing things' when we have the discipline of concentration, and this is linked to the control of our consciousness.

In contrast, procrastination is like putting on the handbrake or treading water; when we procrastinate, we are avoiding what is best for us and what we ought to be doing to help ourselves out. When we procrastinate, we are eating our dessert before our vegetables.

Without labour, nothing prospers.
Sophocles, playwright

I'm fascinated when people say with a resigned expression, 'I'm a procrastinator'. With this statement they seem to accept that this is going to be their approach from there on in; they are not going to *try* to get things done early or on time; there is no point; they are only going to procrastinate. Well, welcome to the club. You are not special or even interesting on this point. We all procrastinate. If you breathe, you procrastinate. Saying 'I'm a procrastinator' is like saying, 'I can't drive', and thinking that this means you will never learn.

Well, it's time to learn. Time to master your habit of procrastination. To be distracted from what you intend to do is a sure sign that you are not in control. It is amazing how little effort we usually put in to improve our control of our attention and concentration. Instead of sharpening our concentration, we put the task aside and turn towards some immediate gratification.

You can reverse the habit through self-inquiry. Ask, 'Why am I putting off this task?' Have a real think about what is happening. Are you thinking you should not have to do unpleasant things? Are you struggling to resist the immediate gratification of (for example) your social media? Do you lack confidence and fear failure, and are you therefore in avoidance mode? Are you used to leaving everything to the last minute and using fear, in the form of deadline, as your motivation, rather than proactive self-will? Do you cram for exams so that if your results are not good you can give the excuse that you just didn't put in the time? This last example is a way of protecting yourself from being vulnerable, because if you really put yourself out there and invest, you might fail. That is scary. I could go on and on.

We also make constant excuses. These are not *reasons* for not applying ourselves to our work; they are *excuses*. It comes down to prioritising, and to the degree of responsibility we take for our inaction. A *reason* is 'I had gastro and spent the night being best friends with the toilet'. An *excuse* is 'I did not have time' – when you did actually have time to watch TV, sleep in, and hang out on social media. If we could live in a world where we were honest with ourselves and others about the true causes for our procrastinating behaviour (I was lacking in motivation, I was scared, I kept going for the easy option, I haven't made time for this), then we could have a constructive conversation about the issue. Instead we live in a world of excuses, which really just means shifting responsibility away from ourselves. If we do not take responsibility for ourselves, we cannot take responsibility for our solutions.

If we can, however, have a stern heart-to-heart with ourselves, we will have more awareness of the hurdles that we are putting up for ourselves. What does the more sensible part of you think? How can you find motivation that will really work for you? For example, for years I procrastinated in getting my monthly tax submissions ready. I have now got this sorted and I get them done early, because I really recognised my desire to not have this dark cloud hanging over me month after month. The pain of not doing it outweighed the pain of getting in and doing it early. I also have built confidence in doing the task, so my insecurity is now calmed and my avoidant behaviour has ended.

A mind trained in concentration builds the skill of seeing exactly what you're choosing to do and not do. It gives you the freedom and the boot in the bum to make better choices. It builds the discipline to make a decision and make it work. You learn not to complain about not getting things done, because whether you get them done or not is your own choosing.

If you see yourself as a procrastinator, be aware that you are not the victim of your procrastination; you have just not taken the reins yet.

> Build your castle before you can enjoy the view.

The mark of a person who is in control of their consciousness is their ability to focus their attention at will. They can remain oblivious to distractions. They can concentrate for as long as it takes for them to achieve their goal. They are able to engage in their **flow** activities – absorbing activities that provide a sense of meaning and purpose – regardless of what is happening externally (for more on 'flow', see Book 3, Part 2). Concentration and avoidance of procrastination help us to extend ourselves and survive in the highly competitive world that we live in.

Concentration is a useful habit, and the sooner you learn it the better. Concentration is like patience. You start out with not much, but then you apply yourself, and over time it stretches and stretches out to last for longer timeframes. Then before you know it you have a decent and useful span of concentration. It is natural to use activities that you find completely absorbing to practise this stretching out of concentration. Because we have chosen to do something that has meaning to us, we are very attracted to this activity, so we will naturally apply ourselves for longer.

Concentration is essential if we are to enjoy living with depth of experience. We feel alive when we develop the habit of finding challenges that bring out our potential for growth. We learn to fill our free time with activities that require our concentration (not procrastination), and this involvement in life leads to a development of our self. We need to search for these avenues of growth; we need to be curious, to be inspired by ideas we hear around us, and to have a mind that is open to broadening our experience of our world. Without this growth, we stagnate. We cannot live on cruise control, because this is not really living.

SOLITUDE

Getting unpleasant work done also often involves spending time on your own and using this alone time well. Instead of escaping from quiet alone time with technology, we need to value and feel comfortable with it. Alone time is especially important if we are mastering a serious mental task, like studying or working on a complex project.

We often avoid this time by ourselves for it can mean making space for negative thoughts about the past or future to creep in. We sometimes dive into social media or TV to avoid this space. These responses are regressive. They do not lead us forward. The way to grow while enjoying life is to take on new challenges as opportunities for learning and for improving skills.

We all want to feel confident. How about we set ourselves up with many skills and strengths to feel confident in? It is a skill to control our attention in solitude, and one worth learning and continuing to strengthen. You cannot take up deeper exploration of your inner reality or the extraordinary untapped opportunities around you if you have not acquired the habit of using solitude to your advantage. When our physical vigour and agility wane with age, we turn our energies from mastery of the external world towards our internal world. We grow our interests, our knowledge and our discoveries about the world around us. We can only transition to this complete celebration of and perhaps reliance on our internal world if we have mastered the skill of concentration and using solitude to our full advantage.

So, learn the arts of concentration and minimal procrastination for the sake of your future, but you will reap the benefits from now on.

SUCCESS

People who succeed – who are at the top of their field – usually get there through working harder than anybody else. While they have a certain amount of talent that separates them, in the end it is their aptitude for hard work and concentration and actually following through on the work that sets them apart. If you're very talented, it's the easiest thing in the world to take that for granted and not work. It's dedication to a job that creates success, and this perseverance is a serious thing; it is not to be taken lightly. We admire this dedication in other people's work and we can be proud of it within ourselves. Don't wait for someone to tell you you're worthy of success; just get out there.

Another great skill that successful people have locked in is efficiency. In other words: working smart. The Pareto Principle states that 80% of our results come from just 20% of our actions. The key is working out which of your efforts are creating the change – having the most impact or producing the most gains – and to focus on this area. This is true efficiency.

So, to use studying as an example, you may find that there is one technique that facilitates most of your learning, so you focus on this. You don't give all of your activities the same time and focus because they are not all equal in their impact. Don't get distracted by areas that don't have impact. With business, try refining the key actions that contribute to the quality of your work, your value and your reputation. Ask: what is the key ingredient that is getting new clients in the door? You then selectively put the majority of your energy into that area. This is another area of self-inquiry that might help you achieve and succeed. This is about auditing the efficiency of your time and effort.

A thriving life is about building, expansion and movement. As we know, building is always slower than destruction, and virtually all things that matter take time. Our contentment, our happiness and our state of flow come from this very *process* of doing things over time. Self-discipline is about knowing that life is not always fun. We cannot always have immediate gratification. Sometimes we need to build our castle before we can enjoy the view.

This is also about our work ethic. It is from the process of building that we get our stories and our sense of accomplishment. Whether it be studying, building a relationship, landscaping, learning an artform, parenting our kids, pursuing our work goals, learning a skill, it usually takes a long time. We are learning new things; we are extending our behaviours. This is where we can demonstrate the highly regarded virtues of patience and determination. We cannot just put our hand out and expect things. We build, we create, and we take great pride, and experience a sense of purpose and a state of flow in the process.

CHAPTER 12
NO ENTITLEMENT

We need to push ourselves to make our lives happen. A happy by-product of our increased emphasis on being more aware of our psychology is having more empathy and sympathy for ourselves and others, which somehow often leads to a softening of expectations of ourselves and others.

I am not talking just about the younger generation. I'm talking across the board, all ages; if the shoe fits. Actually, I believe members of the younger generation are inspiring. They have grown up in a truly technological age, and this has allowed them to have a deepened understanding of the world outside of themselves. It is cool to be smart and informed. I think this is the generation that will tackle environmental issues and won't put up with sexism; they will fight for what is right.

While it is wonderful and essential to have compassion for our vulnerabilities, we must also want the best for each other and ourselves. This means living to our potential, having high standards and expecting ourselves to have a strong sense of responsibility and self-determination. If you have an apprentice working for you, it's great to be compassionate regarding her rough patches in life, but you want her to also learn her craft to a high standard. This is ultimately for her best future. Life is an apprenticeship for figuring out how to be an optimally skilled and happy, contented adult, so why would we not expect high standards of our skills and our performance as an adult? We cannot grow unless we take full responsibility for ourselves and we step up to extend ourselves.

Inspiration comes from hard work.

Unfortunately, there is an epidemic of entitlement in our society. People complain that they do not have what they want in life, as if it should just be given to them. They think they deserve it, or perhaps they just want it. We can often be like children in this regard. We want the castle, but we are not prepared to build it. Perhaps this has come from an over-reliance on the immediate gratification of gaming, technology and social media. Perhaps it is from too much exposure to the meat market on social media or the constant marketing of shiny glamour in traditional media, and not enough airtime given to the reality of hard work, dedication and persistence. Perhaps you could argue that many in the older generations traditionally believed in a hard work ethic. They did not have the option of immediate gratification. Perhaps this is a strength that we can learn from? Inspiration does not come without hard work. It is through hard work that we grow and develop. If you want a rich, deep and profound life, you must work hard; you cannot just expect that it should come to you.

CHAPTER 13
INTERNAL STOCKTAKE: WHAT DO YOU SUBSCRIBE TO?

Our contemporary Western culture in Australia, in general, does not make us feel good about ourselves. We're off track if we go chasing superficial image and status. As these do not give depth of joy or meaning, people who chase them are really chasing their tails, and perhaps not stopping to realise that they do not have the desired pay-off. These people are trying to get a quick fix of happiness or are trying to soothe insecurities – when, really, their insecurities can only be soothed by self-love and nurturing, values that are light years away from superficial image and status.

So, if your culture is teaching you the wrong things, don't buy it. Be strong enough to create your own culture. What do you subscribe to in your life values?

To really come *alive*, we need to examine what it is in life that deadens us. We need to get rid of the dead wood. This is a time to recap and renew. It is about keeping your brain and body active. We don't want to slip into set routines and patterns that give us few new experiences or lessons. Working with people who have recovered from near-death experiences, I have witnessed this reawakening and spring clean in life. We do not have to overcome cancer to have this level of being awake to what is important, however. It is time for a shake up, time for an internal stocktake. What are our out-of-date, stagnant or unhelpful routines? What do we need to get rid of? How do we want to expand? Where do we feel emotional depletion and tiredness?

Having a decent holiday is great for creating a bit of distance to shake up our perspective. We can come back and decide to readjust and update our worlds. This does not mean packing up and cancelling our lives, relationships and work. This does not mean setting ourselves up for being isolated. This means adjusting, refining, growing. If change needs to happen, it is with awareness and a sense of responsibility for one's own part, and through mindfully approaching the problem. This is a time to become healthier in all aspects of life and a time to become even more interesting as a person.

Learn to know, learn to do, learn to be.

Do you want to inject freshness? One really easy way to shake things up is to do the opposite of everything you normally do. Change your experience of your normal daily life. Experience it from a different perspective. Try sleeping at the opposite end of the bed, walk your usual route backwards, go to the gym during a time you never used to, eat dinner for breakfast, go for a random drive or train ride somewhere you've never been. Put on a gown or a suit around the house. You will be amused; it won't be your typical day, and you will have a jolt of freshness. See where your mood and your head go with this.

CHAPTER 14
OPEN PALM

We can only control what we can control: our behaviour. Everything else in life we really have little control over. We can encourage, influence, shape, increase the odds of a positive outcome with our efforts, but in truth, we cannot control others' behaviour, emotions or thoughts, society and world events, the weather, or potential health issues. With all of these variables, we can have a lot of curve balls thrown our way.

So, what do we do here? The answer: we look forward to life with the proviso 'all going well'. Which means, 'I hope to have this outcome, or have the enjoyment or achievement, but I realise that something may go amiss, and I accept that; I am mentally open to it. We may be going on a holiday, and I accept that someone may get sick, we may lose something important, our plans may not work out, we may get on each other's nerves, or there may be problems in the community we are visiting'.

Acceptance that we cannot choreograph life or lock in our expectations allows us to cope, to be more adaptive and to tolerate it when things go wrong. We have left room in our minds that this might happen. We have perhaps prepared ourselves for alternative outcomes. We are just being real. I am not suggesting that we be pessimistic – far from it. We are not saying that it is *likely* to go wrong, but we are just allowing room for the possibility of something difficult popping up and throwing off our plans. 'We plan to have a high-paced holiday, all going well', 'I plan to get this work done, all going well', 'I hope to work through this issue with my partner, all going well', 'I want to finish the painting today, all going well'.

Holding tightly with an open palm.

This is skill of holding life lightly. It is about not grabbing life tightly and assuming that we have control of what is going on around us, when we actually do not. This is called 'holding tightly with an open palm'.

IN CONCLUSION

Life is meaningful, rich and indeed short. The most distinguished skill of all is therefore the art of living life well. We need to nail being fully human, which means being awesome at being an adult. Life is a wonderful learning opportunity. The best of human nature is our capacity to learn and love. May you grow yourself, grow your people, grow your love and grow your intent. May you be compassionate, gentle, courageous and at peace within yourself. I wish you all the best for this adventure.

FURTHER READING

In chapter 10 I referred to *The barefoot investor*. Scott Pape offers some practical and powerful direction on finance; if you're interested in exploring it further, these details will help you:

Pape, S (2020), *The barefoot investor: the only money guide you'll ever need*, John Wiley and Sons Australia, Milton, QLD.

You might also like to refer to the following works to explore some of the concepts in this book further. Mitch Albom shares wise words about life that he learnt from his mentor Morrie Schwartz – words that wake you up and ground you – while John O'Donohue's prose speaks of where we sit in life.

Albom, M (1988), *Tuesdays with Morrie*, Hodder, Sydney.

O'Donohue, J (2008), *To bless the space between us: a book of blessings*, Doubleday, New York.

And, finally, if you wish to explore the topics I have touched on briefly in this book more deeply, you might like to try the other books in the 'Signposts for Living' series by Dr Kirsten Hunter:

Book 1: Control your Consciousness – In the Driver's Seat

Book 2: Understanding Myself – Be an Expert

Book 3: Mindfulness and State of Flow – Living with Purpose and Passion

Book 4: Understanding Others – Loved Ones to Tricky Ones

Book 5: Parenting – Love, Pride, Apprenticeship

ACKNOWLEDGEMENTS

To Jon, my beautiful husband, your support is constant. I can always rely on you to be in my corner, patiently championing me on while I sit typing away. With writing, having someone who believes in you makes all the difference. Thank you that it is always 'us' facing the next challenge, the next hurdle. I love you.

My devoted mum has been the rock through my childhood and every chapter of my adulthood. No child could have a more extraordinary mum. I'm proud of you and I love you.

Our five boys, Lachlan, James, Tobias, Jack, and George, when you heard that your mum was writing books, non-fiction and fiction, your response was simply 'of course she is'. When you heard mum was publishing, your response was 'of course she is'. When we talk about the book being successful in reaching a wide audience, your response, 'of course it will'. You boys are so beautiful. Ever-resounding support, thank you. I love you.

Vanya Lowther, you are the smartest person I know, and perhaps the wisest. You are also my closest and my lifelong friend. Thank you for taking on the mammoth task of being the first person to put your eyes on the *Signposts for Living* books. Your perseverance, your contribution and brainpower was and is so appreciated. I love you.

Jane Smith, I agree with Stephen King, 'to write is human, to edit is divine'. Thank you for your eye for detail, your grammatical wizardry and staying fresh when there was so much work to do. You're a talented gem.

ABOUT THE AUTHOR

Dr Kirsten Hunter is a clinical psychologist with 20 years' experience working with children, adolescents, adults, and couples across the expanse of clinical areas. Between running her private practice, enjoying time with her family, and writing her books, Kirsten juggles a range of passions – particularly for scuba diving and hiking. Kirsten is known for diving deep into life, creating and embracing all of life's opportunities. Born in Brisbane, she now lives in Toowoomba, Australia, with her six men: her husband and their five sons. Even their pets are male ...

www.ingramcontent.com/pod-product-compliance
Lightning Source LLC
Chambersburg PA
CBHW041958080526
44588CB00021B/2793